# The Sacred Heart *of* Jesus

## YESTERDAY, TODAY, FOREVER

Bernard  Häring,  C.Ss.R.

**LIGUORI CELEBRATION SERIES**

Please Do Not Remove
Property Of
The Cenacle of Our Lady
of Divine Providence

Liguori

ONE LIGUORI DRIVE
LIGUORI MO 63057-9999
314.464.2500

ISBN 0-7648-0358-1
Library of Congress Catalog Card Number: 98-67382

© 1999, Munich Province of the Redemptorists
Printed in the United States of America
03 02 01 00 99   5 4 3 2 1

All rights reserved. No part of this book may be reproduced, stored in a retrieval system, or transmitted without the written permission of Liguori Publications.

Scripture quotations from the *New Revised Standard Version of the Bible*, © 1989 by the Division of Christian Education of the National Council of the Churches of Christ in the USA. Used with permission. All rights reserved.

This is a revised edition of a book originally titled *Heart of Jesus: Symbol of Redeeming Love*, © 1983, Liguori Publications.

Cover design by Wendy Barnes

# Table *of* Contents

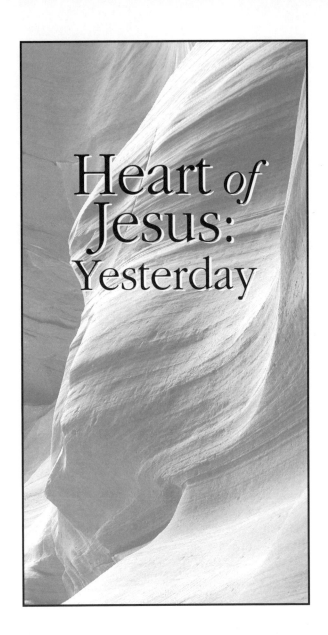

# Heart *of* Jesus: Yesterday

# Veneration *of the* Sacred Heart *of* Jesus

All of humanity—every man, woman, and child—is in dire need of redemption in all its dimensions and on all levels. This is especially true of the innermost self, the heart, which is often wounded, hurt, misguided, disturbed, cold, unyielding. Evil thoughts, desires, plans, and deeds may arise from the heart; but from its deepest depths a longing, a cry for redemption, for liberty and true love, makes its presence felt.

It is in the heart that redemption begins to function and to change the person and the world. Redemption and the healing of persons and their relationships come from God's loving designs and "thoughts of peace." These become actual events whenever they touch the human heart with God's love.

In the heart of Jesus, the love of God tangibly meets us. From his heart arises the perfect response of human love to the Father. Jesus wants nothing less than to flood our hearts with his own overflowing love, thus making us participants in the love of the triune God, present and visible in his Sacred Heart.

Modern godlessness is, above all, a perversion of the human heart. It indicates that we have lost our center; we have gone astray in our inmost being, in our hidden thoughts and desires. "Heart" is a key concept of humanity. Scarcely any other word recurs so often in sacred Scripture. The Bible speaks of the human heart in various ways: as the depth and center of our being, as conscience, as the inmost calling to love, as being created and recreated for redeemed love. The Bible also speaks of the heart of God, revealed simply as Love, in loving deeds and words, in looking at us and drawing our own hearts to transcendence.

Integrity of heart is the guarantee of healthy human relationships. The word "heart" is both a symbolic and realistic expression for knowing lovingly. In everyday language, in popular songs, and in great literature, attention centers on the heart when a person is deeply moved by the love shown by others or by the Other and, equally, if a great love meets rejection or is otherwise distressed.

Devotion to the Sacred Heart of Jesus, as it has evolved throughout the centuries and as proposed by the teaching and liturgy of the Church, is a conscious concentration on both the symbolic and palpable reality of the heart, particularly in the personal encounter of our hearts with the heart of Jesus. In this light, we come to see and to contemplate the whole of revelation as the dynamic, attractive communication of divine love in and through a human heart that is at the same time divine. We also see that our noblest vocation is to be called to love.

True veneration of the Sacred Heart of Jesus is more than just a private devotion tending toward excessive sentimentality. In the heart of Jesus are revealed the love and mercy of God for the salvation of all of humankind. The divine purpose is nothing less than to bring us back to the love of God from which we have gone astray. It is a clear-cut call to an all-inclusive solidarity.

The heart of Jesus tells us of the greatness of God's love for us, but also of how devastating it is for our innermost selves—and for all the world—if this love is refused. Jesus' redemptive love wants to touch and transform us in order to make us the light of the world, a new people with healthy relationships. Those who are seized by the love of Jesus' heart grieve over the sins of the world, and they long for reparation.

With great fervor, the ancient Church Fathers meditated and reflected on the wounded heart of Jesus. They recalled the "beloved disciple" who, at the Last Supper, was nearest to the heart of Jesus. Within this context, they brought together the many texts of the Old and New Testaments which tell of the heart-love of God, the image of God as the Father of Israel, the Divine Physician, the Good Shepherd, the Divine Spouse who, in spite of all our sins, remains faithful to the people God loved into being.

Saint Anselm did much to revitalize this great heritage in his time. Saint Bernard of Clairvaux was also an abiding influence who saw, in the heart of Jesus opened for us, the revelation of the deepest secrets of God.

Great too was the impact of Saint Francis of Assisi. We look to Francis as the disciple of Jesus, so near to the heart of Jesus that he shared with the Beloved Master the wound of his heart and the wounds of his hands and feet. Saint Bonaventure was also a great exponent of this devotion.

Devotion to the Sacred Heart was at its best during the thirteenth century, especially in the monastery of the Benedictine nuns in Helfta, under Saints Mechtilde and Gertrude the Great. There, the contemplation of Jesus' heart, overflowing with love and drawing all sensitive hearts to himself, was the focal point of piety. It drew the hearts of many people to a tender love of Jesus.

History shows that devotion to the Sacred Heart of Jesus and a great love for the Eucharist are inseparable. This is most evident in the lives of Saints Gertrude and Mechtilde. Their devotion to the Sacred Heart was centered in the liturgy. The celebration of the Eucharist inspired them to contemplate and to praise the loving heart of Jesus who, seated at the right hand of the Father, constantly intercedes for us. Jesus, who gave us this memorial of his sacrificial and atoning love, is now present in the Eucharist, bestowing on us the wonderful pledge of the love of his heart. It is especially in the Eucharist that he offers us, as it were, an "exchange of heart," conforming our hearts to his heart.

A happy development came about through a combination of the mystical approach and the sacramental vision promoted by Cardinal Berulle and his school. It peaked with Saint John Eudes, the pioneer of the liturgy of the Sacred Heart of Jesus. He authored liturgical texts for the celebration of the Eucharist and for the breviary in honor of the Sacred Heart, ecclesiastically allowed for use in France in 1668.

The adoration of Jesus in the Eucharist, and union with him in praise of the Father, are at the very center of John Eudes' devotion to the Sacred Heart.

Only with deep sorrow can we think of how many people remain ungrateful, even dishonor the Lord in the Eucharist. John Eudes summoned us to special atonement for all the sins against the loving eucharistic heart of Jesus. This atonement, centered in a grateful and sacrificial love, stands ready to offer everything that love demands in reparation for the sins of ingratitude. John Eudes was well aware that our atonement has value only in union with the sacrifice of Christ, a union of heart and mind that Jesus both invites us to and makes possible for us in the Eucharist.

The spirituality and zeal of Saint Margaret Mary Alacoque for the liturgy of the Sacred Heart followed the same direction as that of Saint John Eudes. This was a new emphasis within a rich tradition, with a particular interest in its liturgical expression. An urgent appeal for expiation of sin and conversion to merciful love are its main characteristics. She was convinced that souls wholly captured by the eucharistic love of Jesus can atone validly, and through their adoring and generous love, can provide a balance for the terrible coldness and hardness of so many hearts.

John Eudes and Margaret Mary Alacoque also helped to overcome Jansenism which, by its rigorism, alienated many Christians from Holy Communion and from trust in the merciful love of the Redeemer.

Some of Alacoque's formulations met with considerable opposition, but the authority of Saint Alphonsus, who himself fervently venerated the Sacred Heart, settled the problem. Some were holding that the heart is the seat of all affection. Alphonsus maintained that such an assertion was contrary to the insights of science and in no way necessary for the purpose and meaning of this devotion. He insisted upon the basic symbolism of the broader concept of "heart," as found in the Bible and Church Tradition. Approbation for public liturgy of the devotion was granted by Clement XIII in 1765.

Saint Alphonsus, a most efficacious protagonist against Jansenistic rigorism and coldness of heart, extolled, in particular, God's loving permanent presence in the Eucharist as a sign of the invincible love of the heart of Jesus. He saw daily visits to the Blessed Sacrament as an expression of grateful memory and of constant praise because Jesus never forgets us.

Alphonsus considered the human memory to be a basic gift, in a sense superior to the intellect and will. Through a grateful memory, God inserts us into the history of salvation, opens to us the treasures of the past, enriches the present, and provides us with the dynamics for future direction.

Saint Alphonsus was a persistent promoter of the practice of frequent Holy Communion. He was convinced that rigorists did not really know the merciful love of the heavenly Father and the loving heart of the Redeemer.

Finding our blissful abode with Jesus in the Blessed Sacrament, indeed in his very heart, helps us to anticipate heaven and provides us with constant guidance on the way to it. In the sacrament of loving union, Alphonsus perceived the Divine Physician, the Good Shepherd who nourishes in us effective and faithful responses of friendship, trust, love, and joy in the nearness of his presence.

We do not go to Communion in order to be rewarded for our virtue. Rather, we joyfully accept the divine invitation because we are aware of the gracious, merciful, and healing love of Jesus and yearn to love him in return. As we receive healing and strength from Jesus, we long all the more to increase our love for him—

and, through him, our love for our neighbor—since he alone is the source of redeemed and redeeming love.

The Dominicans claim a goodly number of fervent promoters of devotion to the Sacred Heart, beginning with Saint Dominic, their founder. Proponents include the Order's greatest theologians, from Saints Albert and Thomas Aquinas to the mystical school of Meister Eckhart and Tauler.

The role of Blessed Henry Suso—who died in 1366—was unique. His love of Jesus' heart, pierced for us all, knew no bounds. A charismatic poet and preacher, he inspired great numbers to practice veneration of the Sacred Heart. In his deep devotion, Suso saw Jesus in his full humanity and strength, one who made himself humble to heal our tendency to pride. In his prayers, Henry frequently spoke to "Divine Wisdom," most loving and most worthy of love. He was overwhelmed by Wisdom's love for us. He exulted when she said to him: *"Be wise, my child, and make my heart glad"* (Proverbs 27:11a). Enraptured, he responded, "I embrace you with my heart's burning longing." His spirituality was one of constant praise of God's mercy, particularly as revealed in Jesus' suffering heart. The desired fruit of this loving praise is a gift of serenity and peace. It allows the true disciple to feel deep compassion and generous love, and to offer whatever sacrifices are required for the sake of God's suffering people.

The writings of Eckhart, Tauler, and especially Suso had a long-lasting influence in France, Italy, and Germany. Many people were reached and touched by this devotion, especially through the influence of Saint Catherine of Siena. These classical promoters of the devotion to the Sacred Heart express salvation-solidarity.

In 1856, Pius IX made the liturgical celebration of the feast of the Sacred Heart of Jesus obligatory in the whole Church. Leo XIII deepened the understanding of consecration to the Sacred Heart, illustrating the relationship between veneration of the Sacred Heart and the salvation of the world.

The doctrinal development of the devotion to the Sacred Heart is summarized in Pius XII's encyclical, *Haurietis Aquas.* In it, he explicitly insists that veneration of the Sacred Heart of Jesus is based soundly and squarely on the Bible and Church Tradition.

We join Jesus in his high-priestly prayer: *"And for their sakes I sanctify myself, so that they also may be sanctified in truth"* (John 17:19). Confident in prayer, we open ourselves to the rich graces of Holy Communion wherein heart reposes in heart. With hearts renewed, we come closer to the beatitude assured to those who are "pure in heart." A grateful memory will then help us to watch over the purity of our motives and intentions.

In the Eucharist, Jesus prepares a festive banquet for his friends, a pledge of the heavenly banquet and everlasting feast of love and joy. Thus we come to a better understanding of his invitation: *"Let everyone who is thirsty come. Let anyone who wishes take the water of life as a gift"* (Revelation 22:17b). And we respond with our hearts: *Come, Lord Jesus!* (Revelation 22:20b).

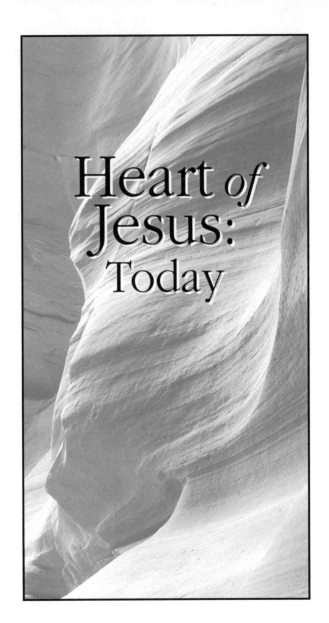

# Heart *of* Jesus: Today

# *Our* Perfect Paradigm

RIVERS OF LIVING WATER

*On the last day of the festival, the great day, while Jesus was standing there, he cried out, "Let anyone who is thirsty come to me, and let the one who believes in me drink. As the scripture has said, 'Out of the believer's heart shall flow rivers of living water.'" Now he said this about the Spirit, which believers in him were to receive; for as yet there was no Spirit, because Jesus was not yet glorified* (John 7:37-39).

*One of the soldiers pierced his side with a spear, and at once blood and water came out* (John 19:34-35).

The symbol of "rivers of living water," which first have to flow from the pierced heart of the Redeemer before they can flow from the believers, is a well-known heritage of our devotion to the Sacred Heart. It is one of its biblical foundations which attracted many hearts. With the opening of the heart of the Redeemer, who with his last breath has entrusted his Spirit to the Father, the first act of glorification of the Father is accomplished. This will be followed by the glorification of the Son, through the Father, in Christ's Resurrection and in the outpouring of the Holy Spirit.

From the fountain of salvation we drink the great gift of redemption, the Holy Spirit, who opens our hearts for redeemed love and fills them from the overflow of boundless love emerging out of the heart of Jesus. *God's love has been poured into our hearts through the Holy Spirit that has been given to us* (Romans 5:5b). Urgently, Jesus invites us to drink from this fountain, not just enough to quench our own thirst but enough to strengthen us to become fountains of saving love for others.

For his encyclical on the Sacred Heart, Pius XII chose as opening words, *"Haurietis Aquas,"* from the text of the prophet: *With joy you will draw water from the wells of salvation* (Isaiah 12:3). This is cause for rejoicing, thanksgiving, and praise: *Shout aloud and sing for joy, O royal Zion, for great in your midst is the Holy One of Israel* (Isaiah 12:6). The image reminds us of Moses, whom God told to summon living water from a rock. And Paul says: *...and all drank the same spiritual drink. For they drank from the spiritual rock that followed them, and the rock was Christ* (1 Corinthians 10:4).

The first thing for us to do, therefore, is to quench our thirst for redeeming love at the fountain of deliverance, as Jesus invited us to do: *"Let anyone who is thirsty come to me"* (John 7:37). The Holy Spirit, through the ministry of salvation in the Church, continues to invite us. All who have tasted the streams of living water eagerly pass on to others this same invitation: *The Spirit and the bride say, "Come." And let everyone who hears say, "Come." And let everyone who is thirsty come. Let anyone who wishes take the water of life as a gift* (Revelation 22:17).

Jesus, who on the cross was both humiliated and exalted, extends to us his abundant love, the source of life. *The Lamb at the center of the throne will be their shepherd, and he will guide them to springs of the water of life* (Revelation 7:17).

The Holy Spirit is the personified gift by which God's self is eternally given to the Word, his Son, and the Word returns God's love and himself as gift to his Father. In his humanity, Jesus is anointed and sent by the Spirit for the work of redemption. In the power of the same Spirit, Jesus offers himself on the cross as a sacrificial gift to the Father for our sake. And with the flow of blood and water from his opened heart, he becomes the fountain of the gift of the Holy Spirit for us.

By the same power of the Spirit through which Jesus has made himself a sin-offering for us, he gives himself in the Eucharist as a source of everlasting love for us. And the glorious circle becomes perfect in that Jesus sends us the Holy Spirit from God to enable us to give our hearts and entrust ourselves to the Father in union with Jesus. Thus do our lives become an expression of grateful love, of lasting praise for such an undeserved gift.

This superabundant redemption manifests itself particularly when those who have quenched their thirst at the fountain of the water of life, and are captured by the love of Jesus, become one with Christ, allowing *"rivers of living water"* to flow out from within them.

The biblical teaching is that no one can have a vital share in the love of the Redeemer without actively joining in his love for all. The gift of the Spirit cannot be buried in a selfish heart. Through unceasing thanksgiving for these gifts, our hearts become more and more fashioned after the heart of Jesus, Redeemer of the world. As a consequence, we urge all who are thirsty to come to Jesus and to drink from his love.

The consecration of ourselves and of the world to the heart of Jesus must be seen in this light. Consecrated by the Holy Spirit to the love of the Redeemer of the world, we consciously accept our mission: *"As you have sent me into the world, so I have sent them into the world. And for their sakes I sanctify myself, so that they also may be sanctified in truth"* (John 17:18-19). Jesus makes it clear that this mission and this consecration come to us as a transforming, renewing power of the Spirit: *Jesus said to them again, "Peace be with you. As the Father has sent me, so I send you." When he had said this, he breathed on them and said to them, "Receive the Holy Spirit"* (John 20:21-22).

What the world most urgently needs is that love which flows from the heart of Jesus, pierced for us and glorified by the Father. The beginning of the way of salvation is to have a great thirst for this love, without which we cannot be *salt of the earth* and *light of the world.* If we are alert to how much the world needs this greatest of all gifts, this awareness will increase our own desires and endeavors.

## Prayer

*Most loving Lord and Master, the terrible thirst which you suffered when you were losing the last drops of your precious blood is a heartbreaking symbol of your thirst to share with us the riches of your love and your redemption. We thank you for constantly inviting us—through your own voice from the cross, through the voice of the "Spirit and the bride," and through the voices of all venerators of your heart—to drink thirstily at the fountain of salvation so that the water of life can flow from within us to others.*

*Send forth your Spirit to awaken in us this thirst. Let your thirst become ours; let your love become our love for all the redeemed, so that all may come to experience this love and become ever more thirsty for a greater love.*

*Lord Jesus, you have told us: "If two of you agree on earth about anything you ask, it will be done for you by my Father in heaven" (Matthew 18:19).*

*We know that we can pray with complete trust if we look at what your heart desires most for us. So we come to pray not for small things but for the greatest of all gifts: that you draw us so much to your heart that we long to see all people drawn to this same love. Then there will be goodness and peace throughout the world, and you can hand us all over to the Father as your gift.*

*Lord Jesus, the blood and water that flowed from your pierced heart on the cross represented streams of salvation for all. We beg you, send us your Holy Spirit to renew our hearts, to cleanse them and inflame them with your love: love for you, love for our brothers and sisters all over the world. Grant us a joyful, grateful, and strong faith; for only from within true believers can the streams of the water of life flow to others.*

## HEART OF JESUS AND GOD'S PEOPLE

*Christ loved the church and gave himself up for her, in order to make her holy by cleansing her with the washing of water by the word, so as to present the church to himself in splendor, without a spot or wrinkle or anything of the kind—yes, so that she may be holy and without blemish* (Ephesians 5:25-27).

The Old Testament shows that God's adoption of a nation is ordered to the people as a whole. Individuals are regarded as "members" of a people. God is the "spouse" of his people. In the New Testament, these images parallel Christ's relationship to his Church. The twelve apostles point to a continuity with the once-united twelve tribes of the chosen people.

The covenant sealed by the blood of the Redeemer, celebrated in the Eucharist, is the covenant of love with the Church. Unlike the former, in this covenant each member is held in his or her own uniqueness. Of course, the Church as a whole points to all of humankind.

Since the time of the Church Fathers, theology has held that the Church is born from the opened heart of Jesus. His heart's blood is its dowry. Jesus, in his overwhelming and faithful love, has chosen the Church out of his own gratuitous love. He has given it life through his redemption, called it into being by his creative word, and bestowed the promise to abide with it until the end of time.

The Church can understand itself, its worth, and its mission only as coming from the love of Jesus Christ. Its first and fundamental task, therefore, is to learn to know and to love Jesus. In this way the Church learns to love all people in union with Jesus' own love. It is the sacrament of salvation insofar as it makes Jesus visible through its members, charisms, ministries, structure, liturgy, and laws. Love should flow from the Church as *"rivers of living water."*

For this purpose, an authentic devotion to the Sacred Heart is most fitting and fruitful. It is a tremendous challenge to the Church and its self-understanding because, in this devotion of devotions, what matters above all is to be touched and moved by the love of the Sacred Heart and to love, with Jesus, the heavenly Father and all the redeemed.

This devotion also prompts an ongoing examination of conscience which looks at the conduct of the entire Church and the lives of each of its members. The result is often a deep sorrow, or even a profound shock that we, as individual members, and the Church as a whole, have responded so poorly to the Love which has chosen us and continues to give us life. Our reaction should lead us to humble penitence and, at the same time, to grateful praise of God's enduring mercy despite our lack of fidelity. But this praise makes sense only when we renew our purpose to respond to this divine fidelity with a steadfast faithfulness.

The Church is meant to be a source of joy for its divine spouse. Jesus exults over those who humbly and gratefully respond to his love. He recognizes all the hidden saints and the many who, in spite of enormous obstacles, are striving for total conversion. He looks with kindness upon the poor sinners who have learned to put all their trust in him. There is great rejoicing in heaven over each of them.

Jesus looks with heartfelt delight on the preaching of conversion through the Church if it is coupled with readiness for ongoing renewal in all aspects of the Church's life. The heart of Jesus welcomes the thrust toward reunion with our separated churches, especially when such efforts are marked by great humility.

But the Church has cost the heart of Jesus many pains. Since he so deeply loved his disciples, their stubbornness and rivalry, their resistance to his real mission as the suffering Messiah often saddened him. Time and again, when he explained his mission to free humankind from pride and arrogance by humble service, his disciples got into disputes over which of them would play the most important role in his reign. Even when Jesus had washed their feet and explained what this was meant to teach them, they refused to accept it. These and many other incidents must have given Jesus a frightening picture of all the troubles his Church would endure from people calling themselves "Christians."

The extreme suffering of Jesus' heart and soul on the eve of his passion was increased by the apathy and sleepiness of his beloved disciples, from whom he should have been able to expect sympathy and consolation. But these are not just past events. They are repeated also in our time, by us, who give so little thought to being a source of joy for all, to the glory of Jesus Christ.

When we look at the heart of Jesus, we should not be tempted to sit in judgment on the Church, forgetting that we are a part of it, partially the cause of its imperfection and distress. We harm the Church by our sin and negligence, hiding its true countenance from people. Jesus must indeed suffer when we dare to pass judgment on his Church.

A deep knowledge and love of Jesus calls for self-criticism of all the Church's members. But if it is really the love of Jesus that seizes and stimulates us, we shall always begin with criticism of ourselves. Our critical awareness of the imperfections of structures and leaders should merge with Christ's mercy and compassion and increase our own striving for holiness.

When we look at the Church in view of Jesus, we shall be ever more gratefully aware of all the good we receive in and from the Church. Realizing how difficult it is for institutional traditions of the Church to change, we praise the Lord that healthy reform has been possible. Especially, we shall praise him for the saints, who teach us by their lives that individual conversion and fruitful commitment for Church renewal are possible when we put our trust in the Lord.

Our relationship with the Church is healthy when we consider everything in light of the love of Jesus for his Church. We see the Church arising from his pierced heart, flowing from it with the blood and water released by the lance. Thus it is clear that we cannot drink from the water of salvation if we bypass the Church, with its ministry of the Word and its sacraments.

## Prayer

*All-loving Savior, we praise you for the great love you have bestowed on your Church. We want to unite ourselves with all the grateful love you have received from your Church, from her saints and penitents. We praise you for your boundless faithfulness and the healing powers flowing from your heart to cure our lack of faithfulness. We unite our sorrow and penitence with all the saintly penitents, past and present, with all who venerate your Sacred Heart, especially those who have offered you atonement in union with the atonement you have offered for us to your Father.*

*We join you in your great and steadfast love for your Church, and learn from you how to love it with your own everlasting love. Help us, by your grace, to gratefully accept our place in the Church, and to serve it faithfully and sincerely.*

*Assist your Church to grow in knowledge and love of your Sacred Heart. Bless it, so that it may be able to lead many people to love you.*

## THE EUCHARISTIC HEART OF JESUS

*Jesus said to them, "Very truly, I tell you, it was not Moses who gave you the bread from heaven, but it is my Father who gives you the true bread from heaven. For the bread of God is that which comes down from heaven and gives life to the world." They said to him, "Sir, give us this bread always." Jesus said to them, "I am the bread of life. Whoever comes to me will never be hungry, and whoever believes in me will never be thirsty"* (John 6:32-35).

History shows that devotion to the Sacred Heart of Jesus and a great love for the Eucharist are inseparable. Jesus, who gave us this memorial of his sacrificial and atoning love, is now present in the Eucharist to bestow on us the wonderful pledge of the love of his heart. It is especially in the Eucharist that he offers us an exchange of heart, conforming our hearts to his heart.

Only with deep sorrow can we think of how many people remain ungrateful and even directly dishonor the Lord in the Eucharist. We are summoned to special atonement for all the sins against the loving eucharistic heart of Jesus. This atonement, centered in a grateful and sacrificial love, stands ready to offer everything that love demands in reparation for the sins of ingratitude. But our atonement can have value only in union with the sacrifice of Christ, a union of heart and mind to which Jesus invites us, and which he makes possible for us in the Eucharist. Finding our blissful abode with Jesus in the Blessed Sacrament, indeed in his very heart, helps us to anticipate heaven and provides us with constant guidance on the way to it.

The most ardent promoters of the liturgical celebration of the mystery of the Sacred Heart have held that this devotion should be seen wholly in light of liturgy, and vice versa. We do not go to Communion in order to be rewarded for our virtue. Rather, we joyfully accept the divine invitation, since we are aware of the gracious, merciful, and healing love of Jesus and yearn to love him in return. As we receive from him healing and strength, we long all the more to increase our love for him—and, through him, our love for our neighbor—since he alone is the source of redeemed and redeeming love.

In the power of the Holy Spirit, Jesus gives himself in Holy Communion with the same love he exhibited when he offered himself up for us on the cross. At the same time, he shares with us the gift of the Spirit to help us return his love and give ourselves totally to him. We ask him to make us wholly his own and to conform our hearts to his heart. Thus his consecrating action becomes reality in our lives.

In the Eucharist, we celebrate the sacrificial love of Jesus—unsurpassable love that he made visible in his bitter passion and death—while praying that this sacrifice might touch and change our hearts and inspire in us a generous and atoning love. As we praise the Father for having prepared this supreme offering made by Jesus once and forever for all of us, our hearts open more and more to the grace that transforms us and makes us an acceptable offering in union with Christ. Gradually, we learn to free ourselves from everything that stands in the way of our union with the sacrificial and atoning love of Jesus.

## LEARNING TO LOVE
## IN THE HEART OF JESUS

*"Abide in me as I abide in you. Just as the branch cannot bear fruit by itself unless it abides in the vine, neither can you unless you abide in me. I am the vine, you are the branches. Those who abide in me and I in them bear much fruit, because apart from me you can do nothing. Whoever does not abide in me is thrown away like a branch and withers; such branches are gathered, thrown into the fire, and burned. If you abide in me, and my words abide in you, ask for whatever you wish, and it will be done for you. My Father is glorified by this, that you bear much fruit and become my disciples. As the Father has loved me, so I have loved you; abide in my love. If you keep my commandments, you will abide in my love, just as I have kept my Father's commandments and abide in his love. I have said these things to you so that my joy may be in you, and that your joy may be complete. This is my commandment, that you love one another as I have loved you"* (John 15: 4-12).

The tender love of Jesus is most personal. It touches everyone in his or her inmost being, in the heart. Yet it may not be privatized. It is an all-out rallying cry. Jesus wants his disciples not only to love him, but also to love—with him—all whom he loves; to love them, as it were, with his own loving heart.

Our first priority is to learn how to love Jesus, to enter fully into the mystery of his loving heart by loving him in return. This is expressed in the basic command: *"Abide in me."* But, immediately and inevitably, there follows the call to *"Love one another!"* This means joining Jesus and his Father in their liberating, redeeming, and healing love for all humankind.

To allow Jesus to conquer our hearts means to enter into the flow of his love. It implies that we *have stripped off the old self with its practices and have clothed [our]selves with the new self, which is being renewed in knowledge according to the image of its creator* (Colossians 3:9-10). The need for grace follows: *As God's chosen ones, holy and beloved, clothe yourselves with compassion, kindness, humility, meekness, and patience. Bear with one another and, if anyone has a complaint against another, forgive each other; just as the Lord has forgiven you, so you also must forgive. Above all, clothe yourselves with love, which binds everything together in perfect harmony. And let the peace of Christ rule in your hearts, to which indeed you were called in the one body. And be thankful* (Colossians 3:12-15).

Saint Thérèse of Lisieux grasped the essence of devotion to the heart of Jesus when she showed her great desire to find her place and role in the Mystical Body by being a loving person in the very heart of Jesus. It is well known that she would have liked to see women ordained as priests, and she wanted to become one of them, but this unfulfilled desire did not ruffle her because she arrived at this alternative: More important than all the ministries and charisms in the Mystical Body is total immersion in the propagation and circulation of love that comes from the heart of Jesus and unites us with his loving heart. This should be the positive desire of every person.

We proclaim the love of Jesus in a trustworthy and understanding manner by loving his own as he did. "His own" are his friends, the believers, those who love him. Those who offend, insult, hate, and persecute their friends drive a lance into Jesus' heart more cruelly than the soldier who on Mount Calvary opened his heart with a lance. Saul—before he became Paul—was doing just that when he was thrown to the ground on the road to Damascus and a voice from heaven asked, *"Saul, Saul, why do you persecute me?"* (Acts of the Apostles 9:4).

But the love of Jesus reaches beyond "his own." He has come to save sinners. He celebrated the messianic meal with tax collectors and sinners. While still on the cross, he prayed for those who had crucified him, for all his enemies. Our devotion to the Sacred Heart becomes sincere and truthful when we learn, from Jesus, to pardon with healing love, and to love the unloving and unloved.

That Jesus' love for us is "costly" is confirmed by his most bitter suffering. We cannot effectively enter into the redeeming stream of his love for others without being conformed to his sacrificial love, without being ready to suffer for love's sake.

It is a lifelong task to learn how to love Jesus and enter into the redeeming stream of his love for all. We should never presume that we have already met the mark. Those who are thoroughly captured by Jesus' love will, like Paul, *press on to make it [our] own, because Christ Jesus has made [us] his own… forgetting what lies behind and straining forward to what lies ahead* (Philippians 3:12b,13b). Friends of the heart of Jesus strive for a love of neighbor that Christ can recognize as his own.

## Prayer

*O most loving heart of Jesus, what fools we are when we concentrate all our energies on garnering different kinds of knowledge and skills, while we strive with only a divided heart for the real wisdom of knowing you and your way of loving people! We confess that in this supreme art we have always remained inept. Yet, thanks to your grace, our hearts are still able to see our folly and perverted sense of proportions. We are deeply pained by our lack of understanding, and in this sorrow we see signs of your gracious patience and forgiveness. So, with your grace, we dare to hope that we shall seek first the reign of your love and all else for your sake.*

*Yet, because we fear our inconsistency, superficiality, and weakness, we implore you, by your loving heart, to confirm our resolve and to increase our desire to seek first your love and the art of loving people in union with your heart. This we ask, no matter what the price may be.*

*Reveal to us the meaning of the Scriptures, so that, like the hearts of the disciples on the road to Emmaus, ours may burn with love for you and with you. Pour out on us your Holy Spirit that we may become a credible community of disciples and the world may believe that the reign of love is at hand.*

## UNION IN THE HEART OF JESUS

*Now the whole group of those who believed were of one heart and soul* (Acts of the Apostles 4:32a).

*"I ask not only on behalf of these, but also on behalf of those who will believe in me through their word, that they may all be one. As you, Father, are in me and I am in you, may they also be in us, so that the world may believe that you have sent me. The glory that you have given me I have given them, so that they may be one, as we are one, I in them and you in me, that they may become completely one, so that the world may know that you have sent me and have loved them even as you have loved me"* (John 17:20-23).

Unity, solidarity, peace, as they come from and lead to God, are matters of the heart—the innnermost being of those who are able and willing to build bridges between people and contribute to the healing of public life.

Nowhere is it written that all had the same ideas, or even that all agreed on solutions to their problems. Even the Acts of the Apostles tell us that there was partial disagreement on some important questions. But the community was *"of one heart and soul."* They met each other in the tender and strong love of Jesus, knowing that Jesus loved them and called them to share in his redeeming, all-inclusive love. They knew that they were sent for a redemptive witness which could not exist without their unity of heart and soul.

This unity of heart bore fruit and led to radical approaches in the conduct of community life. They sought the best possible organizational solutions through gracious dialogue. Everything flowed from their deeply felt solidarity.

The disciples were aware that they were inserted into the supreme mystery of the loving unity between Father and Son. Jesus loves us with the same love as the Father loves us. The Father's love for Jesus is inseparably united with his love for us. In the same way, the love between us cannot be separated from the covenanted love of Jesus for his Church, indeed for the whole of humankind, according to the commission of the Father.

This ineffable mystery marks all of our Christian life. We are authorized to join Jesus, who calls almighty God "Abba," and we are taught by Jesus to call his Father *"our Father,"* thus reminding us that this wonderful prerogative is based on saving solidarity in Christ. We honor the way in which God's Name is glorified when we join in an all-embracing unity and love, in mutual respect and concord.

Without sincere effort toward unity in heart and soul, we can neither hallow the name of God nor greet the coming of the reign of heaven, for we are not yet conformed to God's loving will. God's will is clearly described for us in Jesus' "farewell discourses" (John 17:20-23): that we may all be one as he and the Father are one.

Unity in heart and soul is a stream of living water, arising from within those who believe and have opened themselves to the Spirit sent by Jesus. It is the expression of our vital insertion into the life of Christ. *Let the same mind be in you that was in Christ Jesus* (Philippians 2:5). This is the main perspective and foundation of the counsel imparted to us by Paul: *If then there is any encouragement in Christ, any consolation from love, any sharing in the Spirit, any compassion and sympathy, make my joy complete: be of the same mind, having the same love, being in full accord and of one mind* (Philippians 2:1-2).

Paul's appeal for concord and unity in heart and mind is grounded on the basic truths of our faith. *Lead a life worthy of the calling to which you have been called, with all humility and gentleness, with patience, bearing with one another in love, making every effort to maintain the unity of the Spirit in the bond of peace. There is one body and one Spirit, just as you were called to the one hope of your calling, one Lord, one faith, one baptism, one God and Father of all, who is above all and through all and in all* (Ephesians 4:1b-6).

In this same light, we see the various charisms and ministries for the building up of the Mystical Body of Christ. *The whole body, joined and knit together by every ligament with which it is equipped, as each part is working properly, promotes the body's growth in building itself up in love* (Ephesians 4:16).

## Prayer

*Lord Jesus, most loving and most worthy of love, we thank you for sharing with us your prayer for unity in heart and mind, so that we might live united with your heart and thus glorify the Father.*

*O most gracious heart of our Redeemer, you have suffered terribly at the sight of discord among your disciples, their ridiculous rivalry, their jealousy, and their envy for higher positions. What must your sensitive heart suffer when you see our sloth in matters of mutual love and concord, our laziness in dedicating ourselves to the art of concord in heart and soul, and our failure to learn from you how to love each other as you love us! Forgive us for neglecting to pray zealously for this grace and art which you earnestly desire to grant to those who pray to you sincerely and unceasingly.*

*Lord, open our eyes and our hearts so that we may perceive what is essential. Strengthen our resolution to pray, to act, and to suffer for the great cause of unity among your followers.*

## JESUS, OUR HUMBLE-HEARTED IDEAL

*"Come to me, all you that are weary and are carrying heavy burdens, and I will give you rest. Take my yoke upon you, and learn from me; for I am gentle and humble in heart, and you will find rest for your souls"* (Matthew 11:28-29). Pride and arrogance constrict human hearts and destroy bridges between people. Indeed, they tend to undermine all saving bridges. Pride is the incendiary bomb that destroys. It is the final cause of the heartless devastation resulting from lovelessness and injustice.

Our humble-hearted Savior guides us in the healing of wounded hearts, of painful memories, of alienated relationships, and of difficult human conditions. He builds bridges on which heart discovers heart.

The eternal Word of God chose the path of humility in becoming one of us. He did not come with earthly power and glory; he was born in the misery of a stable.

Jesus washes the feet of his disciples, knowing well how much we need such an example. And the glorified Lord continues to be the great sign of saving humility in the sacraments of faith. He speaks to our hearts and performs his miracles of grace through the humble, earthly signs of the sacraments. Hidden under the sacramental signs, his almighty love is close at hand. In these signs, he continues his humble meeting with us poor sinners until the final revelation of his glory.

What astounding, yet sublime love! God is revealed in the starkest humility, beginning with the incarnation and continuing through to the ignominy of the cross. He makes himself the servant of all. In Jesus' humility, almighty God has shown us the absolute boundlessness of the power of divine love.

But one thing remains forever intolerable to God: pride and arrogance in creatures. *"He has scattered the proud in the thoughts of their hearts. He has brought down the powerful from their thrones, and lifted up the lowly"* (Luke 1:51b-52). In his true humanity, Jesus is the embodiment of the humble ones. Only the humble let God be God in all their lives. Only if we affirm Jesus as the Servant-Messiah can we be healed from the deadly plague of pride.

Jesus calls us. He reaches out to us in our alienation and self-made exile. He yearns to free us from the plague of pride and from the blindness which reflects the pride of the world. His humility is the road that divine love takes from celestial glory to our lowliness. It is Jesus' way to our hearts and the astonishing revelation of his heart. It is also the signpost for our journey on the road to redemption and to everlasting life with God.

Through his humility, the Redeemer shows us how to find rest for our hearts, and how to become a source of peace, kindness, and heartfelt compassion for many people.

As believers, our basic requirement is to find the courage to learn from Jesus the supreme art of loving humility and humble love, whatever the cost. Christ-like love *is* humble; we learn this from the heart of Jesus. The more we love Jesus, the more his secret of humility becomes accessible to us. The more eagerly we learn humility and gentleness, the more Jesus can reveal to us the mysteries of his heart. Gradually, we find peace for our souls, and experience ever more the blessings of humility for ourselves and for others.

## Prayer

*Dear Lord and Savior, we come to you burdened and oppressed by many worries and exhausting labor, by the unbearable yoke that we impose upon ourselves because of our lack of humility. It is a burden we deserve, but it is also the heavy yoke of a sinful world, of collective pride and arrogance. We are bound together in this lamentable condition. We groan and sigh, realizing our plight in this double slavery. What relief we find when we listen to your invitation: "Come to me!" We dare to come.*

*The more we meditate on the crushing burdens you carried in your humility, the more we are filled with grateful wonder. In your divine glory and your human humility you are totally Other, the only true God. You come to us, whose vanity and pride are intolerable, on the royal road of humility. You show us that this is the way to you and to the heart of your Father, the way to the hearts of our neighbors, the way of salvation.*

*Humble heart of our divine Master, we want to learn from you, day by day, the royal way of humility. Your love will be our teacher. Transform our hearts. Make them mirror images of your own heart, fountains of healing for many. Lord, make us humble.*

## LOVE CONQUERS ALL

*Who will separate us from the love of Christ? Will hardship, or distress, or persecution, or famine, or nakedness, or peril, or sword? As it is written, "For your sake we are being killed all day long; we are accounted as sheep to be slaughtered." No, in all these things we are more than conquerors through him who loved us. For I am convinced that neither death, nor life, nor angels, nor rulers, nor things present, nor things to come, nor powers, nor height, nor depth, nor anything else in all creation, will be able to separate us from the love of God in Christ Jesus our Lord* (Romans 8:35-39).

Love is the only absolute power in heaven and on earth. But salvation becomes effective only when we gratefully receive and respond to divine love. This most free gift of God cannot be forced upon any person.

Love found its most perfect dwelling place on earth in the heart of the God/man, Jesus Christ. Jesus came to win us over to love's salvific cause. The heart of Jesus proved itself victorious against all assaults, and brought home to his Father our thankful love.

To his last heartbeat, Jesus fought for love's victory. Crucified, Jesus prayed for his torturers and slanderers. Humiliated, he makes one of the criminals crucified with him the first to be brought home by him to the eternal celebration of the victory of love.

Those faithful ones who stood beneath Jesus' cross saw Jesus' heart, pierced by the soldier's lance, flooding the sinful world with the saving bath of water and blood. After his Resurrection, they were privileged to see the glory of his opened heart. Thomas was even allowed to touch it with his hand. For all believers, this heart is the great sign of God's victory and the sure promise of final conquest.

At the very moment when Jesus reached the most abject point of humiliation and disdain, he was already exalted. He had begun to draw to his heart all those whom God had given him. The firm and faithful hope for love's final conquest constitutes the very substance of Christianity. The cause of love for which Christ came is indeed worth all dedication, even all suffering.

This victorious love is unqualified grace, an undeserved gift flowing from the heart of the Redeemer. But love looks for grateful hearts ready to enrich the hearts of others. There is nothing we can pray for with greater confidence than for this love. The heart of Jesus is the certain assurance that he himself is longing to bestow on us this best of all his gifts. We ask for it in humble and persevering prayer, for we can receive it only if we recognize God as God, the source and goal of all love, and also recognize how much we need this absolutely undeserved gift. Praying for this love which conquers all, we encounter the innermost longing of the heart of Jesus, and indeed of his heavenly Father.

Newly born of grace and trusting completely in God, we can say with Paul: *"I can do all things through him who strengthens me"* (Philippians 4:13). When our hearts yearn for this water of life, then even our weaknesses cannot frighten us. We know that our power to conquer comes from God alone. The final victory of Love is expressly foreshadowed for us if we love those who are unloved and those who offend or despise us, if we sow love where there is hatred, and if we strive to win others to the reign of love visible in the heart of Jesus.

## Prayer

*Most loving Master, your heart is the trophy of history's greatest triumph. The surge of hatred is thwarted by your love. All who refuse your love are like chaff blown away by the wind; and yet you do not write them off. As long as they live, you will seek them and invite them to the banquet celebrating your love for them.*

*O divine heart, filled with love, you have won our hearts. You have dilated, enlivened, and enriched them with your most powerful gift, your gracious and attractive love. To you we entrust ourselves.*

*The world seeks to entice us with dreams of success and vain conquests. Help us to be vigilant in the fight against these seductions. Grant us wisdom, so that we may have only one thing in mind: the victory of your love in our hearts.*

*It is good that we experienced our own painful weaknesses, for now nothing remains but to put our trust in you. Realizing and acknowledging that we can do nothing to save ourselves, we do trust in you. Our hearts are made for abiding love. Your saving love needs witnesses whose hearts have become fountains of its "living water." Increase our faith in your love and our trust in its final victory.*

## JESUS' LOVE SETS US FREE

*Jesus said to the Jews who had believed in him, "If you continue in my word, you are truly my disciples; and you will know the truth, and the truth will make you free." They answered him, "We are descendants of Abraham and have never been slaves to anyone. What do you mean by saying, 'You will be made free'?" Jesus answered them, "Very truly, I tell you, everyone who commits sin is a slave to sin. The slave does not have a permanent place in the household; the son has a place there forever. So if the Son makes you free, you will be free indeed"* (John 8:31-36).

There are two great questions that perturb all thinking people today: "What is truth?" and "What is true freedom?" The two are inseparable. Jesus came to reveal the saving and liberating truth. In a wholly new way, he has restored to humankind the original gift of freedom. The renewed freedom of the redeemed receives its meaning and strength from the love of Christ.

*Christ Jesus…though he was in the form of God, did not regard equality with God as something to be exploited, but emptied himself, taking the form of a slave, being born in human likeness. And being found in human form, he humbled himself and became obedient to the point of death—even death on a cross. Therefore God also highly exalted him and gave him the name that is above every name, so that at the name of Jesus every knee should bend, in heaven and on earth and under the earth, and every tongue should confess that Jesus Christ is Lord, to the glory of God the Father* (Philippians 2:5-11).

Probably the oldest known Christian hymn, this is
a liturgical praise of the amazing liberty of the Son
of God. The hymn points to Christ's Resurrection,
which finally reveals a unique freedom and the
dynamics of love. So we learn from Jesus' heart what
true freedom is.

Jesus sees himself and his freedom as gifts from God.
In gratitude, he freely gives himself back in purest love
and loving service. His freedom proves to be the source
 of boundless freedom to love us with divine and
human love. Through our sinfulness, we are the
unloved and unloving, but thanks to the absolute freedom of Christ we know that we *are* loved. In the power
of his Spirit, we can share in his love for his Father and
for our brothers and sisters.

The self-giving love of Jesus is the great historical
event of liberation. In his full humanity, Jesus "fulfills"
the new law of liberty, the perfect law of love.
Empowered by the Holy Spirit, we are enabled to live
on the same level of freedom. Thus redeemed, we
offer never-ending praise to God, who alone has set us
free: *Thanks be to God through Jesus Christ our Lord!*
(Romans 7:25a).

This freedom is new life, *for the law of the Spirit of
life in Christ Jesus has set you free from the law of
sin and of death* (Romans 8:2). With this new life
comes a new outlook: *To set the mind on the flesh is
death, but to set the mind on the Spirit is life and
peace* (Romans 8:6).

When we entrust ourselves to Christ as he entrusted
himself to his Father, we are at home in his loving heart.
We share his liberating outlook. We are free for each
other and can enjoy all the gifts of God as signs of

liberating love—gifts destined also to become signs of mutual love.

Accepting that freedom of Christ by which he entrusted himself to his Father in the service of all, we are freed from agonizing slavery. We learn to serve God out of grateful love. *God is love, and those who abide in love abide in God, and God abides in them. Love has been perfected among us in this: that we may have boldness on the day of judgment, because as he is, so are we in this world* (1 John 4:16b-17).

Jesus' freedom is not only a freedom-to-be but the supreme freedom-to-be-for-others. With Christ, we conform our will to God's will. This is a source of joy for all of creation, for *the creation itself will be set free from its bondage to decay and will obtain the freedom of the glory of the children of God* (Romans 8:21). Our growth in solidarity and freedom is in the interest of the world for which we are meant to be a shining light.

Having entrusted ourselves to Christ, we are also free from fear of death. *Living is Christ and dying is gain* (Philippians 1:21). The more we find our abode in Jesus' heart, the greater will be our joy when he calls us to be with him forever.

The measure of our freedom arises from the measure of our lives with Jesus. Christian freedom is a light enkindled by the fire of Christ's own love. Inflamed by Jesus' love and inspired by his life, we live lives of service to our neighbor and the world.

## Prayer

*Most loving heart of Jesus, burning hearth of
sacrificial love, we worship you and join you in
praising God for the greatest and all-embracing
gift of love. Created by and for your love, O
Eternal Word of the Father, we have received
gracious redemption which enables us to love you
and, with you, to love our sisters and brothers in
the freedom of adopted children of God. We praise
you and the Father, in the Holy Spirit, for your
infinite freedom to love us so much.*

*We dishonor your great gift of freedom when we
do not render thanks for it. In our foolishness, we
set out to test and prove our own freedom, even in
rebellion against your loving will. In this false
freedom, we leave your Father's house to go into
exile and self-imposed slavery—a slavery which
we prolong every time we use our freedom against
you. Then, as miserable slaves of perverted
self-love, we place ourselves in a position of
becoming unable to love you.*

*O Word of God, breathing the Spirit of love from
all eternity, you shouldered all our miseries except
the greatest one: our incapacity for true love. Yet,
our incapacity made you to suffer, and you did
this out of compassion, in unrestricted freedom to
bear our burden. We can never marvel enough at
your boundless love for us.*

*Source of all freedom and love, open our eyes.
Help us to understand that all talk and effort for
liberation are in vain unless we gratefully allow
you to make us free for your love. Help us to seek
first of all the reign of this loving freedom. Thus
we pray, O Lord, make us free!*

## HEART OF JESUS,
## HEALER OF OUR HEARTS

*I bow my knees before the Father, from whom every family in heaven and on earth takes its name. I pray that, according to the riches of his glory, he may grant that you may be strengthened in your inner being with power through his Spirit, and that Christ may dwell in your hearts through faith, as you are being rooted and grounded in love. I pray that you may have the power to comprehend, with all the saints, what is the breadth and length and height and depth, and to know the love of Christ that surpasses knowledge, so that you may be filled with all the fullness of God* (Ephesians 3:14-19).

The Greek word which we translate as "be converted" is *metanoeite*. It means a whole new way of thinking, feeling, longing—a new, renewed heart. The good news is that now the promised time has come; the time when God, by the power of the Spirit, will create in us a new heart.

This wondrous healing cannot happen through a mere imperative of new laws and external structures in our world. It happens through faith. We allow the good news to take hold of us, and we entrust ourselves totally to God who, in Jesus, opens the treasures of his love for us. Eye to eye and heart to heart with Jesus, we become new people. We think, feel, yearn, and love differently. We see God through the eyes of grateful love. We arrive at a knowledge of what is good, true, and beautiful, accessible only to a heart renewed in love.

Those who have venerated the Sacred Heart through the centuries communicate this truth in various ways. Cardinal Newman, for instance, was inspired by the image of Saint John reposing on Jesus' heart, "until heart in heart repose [and] heart speaks to heart." Others have spoken of the "arrow of love," coming from Jesus' heart and piercing our own; a flame of love that wounds, and at the same time heals, the heart. Some have spoken of an "exchange of hearts" that is offered by Jesus to those who yearn for his love.

Saint Augustine called Jesus the "joy of the pure heart," in the same sense that Jesus calls "blessed" those whose hearts are pure, *"for they will see God"* (Matthew 5:8b). Touched and purified, they see with "eyes of love." By knowing God "with the heart," we are configured to the heart of Jesus, who wants us *to be holy and blameless before him in love* (Ephesians 1:4b).

In Scripture, the word "heart" frequently means a conscience sensitive to God's calling and to everything that is good; a conscience guided and illumined by love. For Christians, this means knowing Jesus lovingly and considering everything in the sight of God. It implies the exercise of saving solidarity by those whose hearts have been won by the love of the Redeemer. With this new heart, we arrive at higher levels of discernment. We begin to think as members of the family of God.

All this powerful attraction and transformation is grace, insertion into the life of Christ. Jesus tells us: *"No one can come to me unless drawn by the Father who sent me; and I will raise that person up on the last day"* (John 6:44); and, *"All things have been handed over to me by my Father; and no one knows who the Son is except the Father, or who the Father is except the Son and anyone to whom the Son chooses to reveal him"* (Luke 10:22).

Entering into the realm of truth and love through the portal of Jesus' heart, being at home in this loving heart, reposing beside Jesus, we develop a new kind of conscience. Everything appears in a new light, has new beauty. Every virtue and every law of God acquires its proper place in the whole picture and becomes attractive. Our conscience becomes alert for the signs of the times, for what the present hour offers, and for the many opportunities to give testimony for Christ and his reign.

This change of heart and conscience can be seen in light of Jesus' words: *"Come to me, all you that are weary and are carrying heavy burdens, and I will give you rest. Take my yoke upon you, and learn from me; for I am gentle and humble in heart, and you will find rest for your souls. For my yoke is easy, and my burden is light"* (Matthew 11:28-30).

The assault of our passions, our slavish fears, and our anguish cease when we repose near the heart of Jesus. We feel new strength, new joy in doing God's will, acknowledging it as an invitation to live as beloved and loving children, as intimate friends. As a result, the decisions of our conscience become more confident, creative, and generous.

In accord with the biblical meaning of "heart," we may also say that reposing in Jesus' heart affects even our unconscious—and our subconscious—life. Not even the best psychotherapists can liberate our conscious and subconscious psychic life as surely as does a new heart-to-heart relationship with Jesus. Rapt in the love of Jesus, a grateful memory opens new avenues for grasping present opportunities, for reshaping past tendencies, and for opening creative doors into the future.

Jesus tells us: *"Out of the abundance of the heart the mouth speaks"* (Matthew 12:34b); and, *"Where your treasure is, there your heart will be also"* (Matthew 6:21). Drawn by the love of Christ, the depth conscience, like a magnetic needle, will point to a clear orientation of life.

The insights of depth psychology about the great importance of our unconscious and subconscious forces are far from being a denial of freedom. When we learn to heal our memories, and to fill them with thankfulness and loving attention—when we allow Jesus to conquer our hearts for his love and for loving our neighbor with him—our souls will find rest.

## HEART OF JESUS THE GOOD SHEPHERD

*"I am the good shepherd. I know my own and my own know me, just as the Father knows me and I know the Father. And I lay down my life for the sheep. I have other sheep that do not belong to this fold. I must bring them also, and they will listen to my voice. So there will be one flock, one shepherd. For this reason the Father loves me, because I lay down my life in order to take it up again"* (John 10:14-17).

The symbol of the "good shepherd"—and Jesus' testimony to it—found an echo similar to that of the later symbol of the "heart." When the good shepherd speaks, it is really the heart of Jesus speaking. He expresses a kind of mutual knowing between the good shepherd and his sheep, between him and his disciples, which he compares with the loving knowledge between himself and his heavenly Father. It is a knowledge of the heart. The self-giving love of which he speaks is the same love which the pierced heart of Jesus continues to speak from the cross.

Emphasizing this same symbol of the good shepherd in his heart-revealing prayer at the Last Supper, Jesus speaks of the peaceful unity of the redeemed. Both the symbolism of the shepherd and the reality of the loving heart of Jesus, forever beating for us, inspire apostolic zeal and dedication to the cause of peace and unity in all genuine disciples of Christ.

After his Resurrection, Jesus questions Peter three times about Peter's love for him. Following Peter's humble, stumbling assurance of his love, Jesus—in gracious confirmation of Peter's supreme office as good shepherd—makes the threefold appeal: *"Feed my lambs....Tend my sheep....Feed my sheep"* (John 21:15c, 16c, 17c). Peter is the prototype. All apostolates, all pastoral activity can be fruitful and truthful only when they arise from humble and loving hearts.

Paul expresses this truth in a way that directly reminds us of Jesus' tender love for the redeemed. *God is my witness, how I long for all of you with the compassion of Christ Jesus* (Philippians 1:8). It is simply impossible to enter intimately into the love of the Redeemer without being seized by his zeal for the salvation of all. It is the vocation of all believers to be an active part of the Church which is an apostolic community. Being enraptured by the loving heart of Jesus is the necessary key to the apostolate. Thus captivated, we bear each other's burdens, encourage and kindly correct one another, and enkindle in many hearts a great enthusiasm for the divine Redeemer and his ongoing work here on earth.

Jesus, who died for all and is risen for all, considers all people—every man, woman, and child—as his own. If he calls us to share in his love and mission as the Good Shepherd—one who knows his own and wants to lead all into the one flock—then nothing can divert us from the wonderful and urgent vocation to make Jesus known and loved.

Humankind is exposed to the most atrocious threats of violence, exploitation, hatred, manipulation, even nuclear destruction. We need nothing more urgently than recognition of the saving message of the Good Shepherd who knows how to guide and protect us. Why should we not have the courage to warn people into what an abyss they will plunge if they refuse the saving love offered them by Jesus? If we have not this courage, if we do not feel the urgency to proclaim the Gospel and give witness to it for the salvation of humankind, we have not yet allowed Christ to captivate us by his love and to conform us to his heart.

## Prayer

*Lord Jesus, you are the Good Shepherd already foretold in the Old Testament. In this, you have shown us the Father. Your love knows no bounds. Even should we run away and go hopelessly astray, still you want to find us and heal us. O Good Shepherd, make us grateful for such a great love and loving care. May gratitude inspire us to accept generously and joyfully your invitation to share in your mission as good shepherds.*

*Heart of Jesus, instill your love into the hearts of all who share in the ministry of shepherds in the Church, and in the hearts of those whom you have chosen for this sublime vocation. Teach them, through your Spirit, how to become true images of you.*

*Send workers into your vineyard. Reawaken the spirit of shepherds who are full of enthusiasm; who radiate joy, peace, kindness, and loving care. Give priests the special charism to inspire apostolic zeal in the hearts of the faithful, so that all may realize what a great honor and joy it is to participate in your mission as good shepherd. Help husbands and wives to become, for each other, true images of your kind, patient, and healing love. Grant to parents the wisdom and strength to raise their children in your love, and to join you in the work of salvation.*

*Lord Jesus, you have spoken exultantly of those believers who "know" you in a way similar to the way you know the Father. Grant to us, from your most loving heart, a firm grasp of this essential point, so that we do not desire anything more than to know you lovingly and to grow constantly in this love and knowledge.*

## HEART OF JESUS THE DIVINE PHYSICIAN

*The Pharisees and their scribes were complaining to his disciples, saying, "Why do you eat and drink with tax collectors and sinners?" Jesus answered, "Those who are well have no need of a physician, but those who are sick; I have come to call not the righteous but sinners to repentance"* (Luke 5:30-32).

*Jesus went throughout Galilee, teaching in their synagogues and proclaiming the good news of the kingdom and curing every disease and every sickness among the people. So his fame spread throughout all Syria, and they brought to him all the sick, those who were afflicted with various diseases and pains, demoniacs, epileptics, and paralytics, and he cured them. And great crowds followed him from Galilee, the Decapolis, Jerusalem, Judea, and from beyond the Jordan* (Matthew 4:23-25).

The title of "divine physician," by which Jesus was honored in early Christianity, is more than a symbol—even as language about the "heart" of Jesus is more than symbolic. These titles signify a deep reality which embraces inexhaustible symbolic riches. Jesus is a healer more so than any human physician. He alone can restore full health and wholeness to body and soul.

From beginning to end, the public activity of Jesus is marked by his healing ministry. When taken prisoner, he lovingly healed the ear of the high priest's servant wounded by Peter. From the cross, he healed the heart and soul of the criminal crucified with him. And this is only the prelude. From the pierced heart of our Redeemer flow continual streams of healing graces. The old Germanic word for "Savior," still much used, is

*Heiland.* It means the One who brings—at one and the same time—salvation and healing. Jesus has come to make us whole and holy.

Jesus is the merciful Samaritan who, faced with the poor man fallen into the hands of robbers, is moved by compassion and takes loving care of the victim at his own expense. We are included in this parable. In the misery of our sins and all the sufferings that derive from them, we are welcomed by the most compassionate Physician.

The wound in Jesus' heart continues to send forth streams of salvation. Jesus welcomes us with gentleness, kindness, healing compassion. His heart remains open for us as a fountain of salvation.

Jesus' benign compassion informs us that healing presumes sincere conversion on our part. Jesus cannot but hate the sin, but he looks at the sinner as a poor brother or sister who has foolishly chosen the darkness of exile. He calls sinners back to wholehearted friendship, offering a new—a loving—heart and a grateful memory.

In accord with Christ's mission, proclamation of the Good News and call to conversion and healing are inseparable. When Jesus proclaims the gospel of the Beatitudes as gift and call, a healing power of love goes out from him. But Jesus, being one with the Father, cannot stay aloof on the Mount when he sees our misery. He comes down from the height to heal people burdened with guilt and suffering. *He came down with them and stood on a level place, with a great crowd of his disciples and a great multitude of people from all Judea, Jerusalem, and the coast of Tyre and Sidon. They had come to hear him and to be healed of their diseases; and those who were troubled with unclean spirits were cured. And all in the crowd were trying to touch him, for power came out from him and healed all of them* (Luke 6:17-19).

If we are yearning to be freed from evil spirits—from self-righteousness, idolatry of status or money, hardness of heart—and if we desire to be cured of other moral diseases, then we must equally yearn to listen to Jesus and to let the Good News enter our hearts. He, who is flooding us with his healing love in the Beatitudes, also shows us the way to heal hearts, to heal human relationships, and to heal public life.

A decisive condition for being healed and becoming true sharers in Jesus' healing ministry is to conform ourselves to his compassionate love. *"Blessed are the merciful, for they will receive mercy"* (Matthew 5:7). Jesus teaches us by word and example what true mercy and compassion mean. He told the Pharisees: *"Go and learn what this means, 'I desire mercy, not sacrifice.' For I have come to call not the righteous but sinners"* (Matthew 9:13). In this context the expression "righteous" means those who meticulously observe certain details of their interpretation of law while looking down on others with disdainful hearts. They are not longing for healing; indeed, they stubbornly turn away from God's healing mercy. They offer unreal sacrifices and refuse the real sacrifice of overcoming their arrogance and renouncing everything that hinders compassionate healing.

By his infinite compassion and merciful actions, Jesus turns our hearts to God: *"Be merciful, just as your Father is merciful"* (Luke 6:36). With Paul, who has wonderfully experienced God's mercy, we all are to praise *the God and Father of our Lord Jesus Christ, the Father of mercies and the God of all consolation* (2 Corinthians 1:3).

When our hearts beat in harmony with the heart of Jesus, we will pardon our adversaries from the depths of our hearts and welcome them with healing love. We concentrate less on our own needs and more on the needs of others.

Paul gives us an attractive picture of redeemed and redeeming love when he says: *Love is patient; love is kind; love is not envious or boastful or arrogant or rude. It does not insist on its own way; it is not irritable or resentful; it does not rejoice in wrongdoing, but rejoices in the truth* (1 Corinthians 13:4-6). Love, flowing from the heart of Jesus and from the heart of the disciple transformed, *is* kind, *is* patient.

Those who learn mercy from the loving heart of Jesus have a new understanding of God's saving justice. They hunger and thirst that God's saving justice may prevail. They commit themselves to work for solutions to world conflicts, not *just* as a matter of justice, but *also* as a matter of compassion.

## Prayer

*O heart of our Redeemer, you have shown us the God of compassion and saving justice. Your heart goes out to all who are in need. We hope to praise your mercy, and that of your heavenly Father, in all eternity. Help us in our commitment to mercy and saving justice.*

*Lord Jesus, we live in a world with many hardened hearts and threatening conflicts. Corruption constantly tempts us, and we cannot deny that we are already partially corrupted. Lord, heal us and make us effective signs of your healing mercy and justice.*

*Divine Savior, send into our estranged world disciples who will steadfastly and straightforwardly bring the gospel of mercy and peace.*

*O heart of Jesus, touch the wealthy, affluent nations, groups, and individuals with a ray of your compassionate love and your zeal for saving justice, so that they may learn what kind of justice you and your heavenly Father want from them.*

*O meek and powerful heart, you can heal our hearts from coldness and sloth and make us a blessing for many people by our deep repentance and conversion. Lord, let this happen soon!*

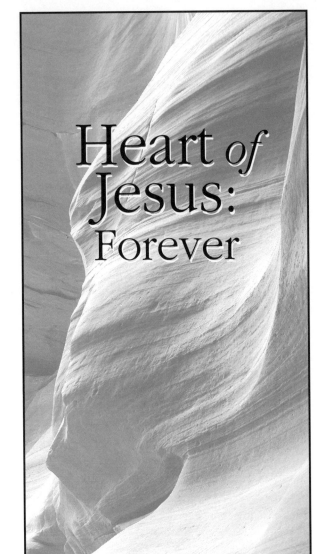

# Heart *of* Jesus: Forever

# Source *of Our* Hope

*"Where, O death, is your victory? Where, O death, is your sting?" The sting of death is sin, and the power of sin is the law. But thanks be to God, who gives us the victory through our Lord Jesus Christ. Therefore, my beloved, be steadfast, immovable, always excelling in the work of the Lord, because you know that in the Lord your labor is not in vain* (1 Corinthians 15:55-58).

The Passover feast has found its fulfillment in the passage of Jesus through the blood-red sea of suffering and death, culminating in the victory of the Resurrection, the triumph of love. His death is a totally new event, transforming the meaning of death for believers. It becomes *Pascha,* the passing over to the fullness of life.

The mystery of redemption is Christ in his Passover. He is revealed as *"the one whom the Father has sanctified and sent into the world"* (John 10:36). Further, he is our wisdom and our virtue, our holiness and our freedom. In death, Jesus is totally seized and consecrated by the holiness of his heavenly Father. He is the forever-accepted sacrifice, the abiding intercessor for the redeemed. The wound in his heart remains as the open fountain of salvation for all who turn to him.

Jesus' death is the supreme prayer, adoration in spirit and truth, manifestation of trust and love, sacrifice of praise and intercession. Living and dying in Christ becomes the Christian way of prayer, total openness for the living water flowing from the heart of Jesus.

Jesus longs intensely to impart to us the riches of his redemption. His heart is widely opened for us. His death has been the supreme fulfillment of his intercession for us, and its acceptance by God is sealed by Christ's Resurrection. Thus the heart of the risen and glorious Christ is the abiding assurance that God, wanting to lead us through death and resurrection to our final home, urgently invites us to conform ourselves with the prayer of Jesus.

Scripture tells us that Jesus died at three in the afternoon. In Israel, this was the privileged hour of prayer, of the evening sacrifice in the Temple. From that point in time, Jesus took over as the never-ending hour of prayer and the acceptable sacrifice.

This sheds abundant light on what is meant by praying "in the name of Jesus." We pray truly in his name if we widen our hearts to conform to the will of the Father as Jesus did and if, out of love for God and neighbor, our persevering prayer becomes an all-embracing desire for the redemption of all. Believers must find their abode in Jesus' heart, longing to pray as he did, indeed, longing to *become* prayer as he did, in order to pray truly "in the name of Jesus."

The paschal mystery of the death and Resurrection of Christ is the center and heart of salvation history. Hence, it should be the center of our own lives. The basic dimensions of our being at home in Jesus' heart, and thus in his paschal mystery, are:

• ***Grateful remembrance*** *of Jesus' painful passover through the sea of suffering.*

• ***Living in the presence of Jesus here and now,*** *in vigilance and openness to him who has come, and comes here and now.*

• ***Hope-filled expectation*** *and clear direction on our road to final homecoming in the heart of our Redeemer.*

In a moving symbol of heartfelt friendship, Scripture enables us to consider our lives in Christ as an invitation to the eternal banquet of love and bliss. We are Jesus' invited guests, friends of the bridegroom. The celebration of the Eucharist reminds us of this nearness to Christ, and thus strengthens within us a grateful memory and watchful readiness.

If we live up to our insertion into salvation history with Christ—by grateful remembrance of past benefits, watchful readiness for present opportunities, and sound foresight for the coming life—the Lord will grant us special gifts to make this journey for which Christ is both our way and our goal: the gifts of discernment, serenity, and above all, peace and joy in his love.

# Prayer

*O loving Redeemer, most worthy of all our love, we feel a deep longing for a most intimate union with you; yet we know that your desire to see us totally united with you is infinitely greater, since it is the expression of pure love. Our desire is still marked by inconstancy, but your wish to grant us the full experience of your friendship is constant and faithful. Lord, purify and strengthen our longing for total love and dedication to you. Widen our hearts! Fill us with your love!*

*We thank you, divine Master, for fully activating praise, thanksgiving, and intercession in our name. Send forth your Spirit, transform us, help us to be so united with you that we can truthfully pray in your name.*

*Lord, help us to overcome the distractions caused by our superficiality. Grant us grateful memories, so we can faithfully meditate on all that you have done and suffered for us. Awaken us from lethargy and let us not forget that you have written us into your loving memory.*

*Lord, help us to be vigilant, ready and able to recognize your coming and your invitation to join you. Give us keen eyes to see more clearly the steps we must take to reach our final goal.*

*Fill our hearts with supreme confidence in your graciousness. Give us serenity in the vicissitudes of life. Make us long to be forever at home in your heavenly kingdom.*

*Lord, make us one with your Passover so that we can look forward to the hour of our death, to our passing over into our abiding home. Free us from anguish and slavish fear. Grant us the grace of perseverance and joyful acceptance when you come to call us home to you.*

# Source *of Our* Joy

The liturgy of the Sacred Heart of Jesus is, above all, an invitation to joy in the Lord. Jesus wants to see us rejoice in his love. If we truly believe in the wholly divine and wholly human love of Jesus and in our being invited to the banquet of love and joy in our eternal abode in Jesus' heart, then surely our hearts exult for joy. Everyday troubles will not deprive us of our serenity and peace if our hearts are joyful. Indeed, all our personal sufferings are trifling compared with the love which the Lord has manifested to us and the happiness he holds out to us.

Lovers find joy in their mutual love and presence to each other. How much greater must be our joy to know that he, who by nature is Love and has shown us his boundless love, really longs for our love in return. Indeed, he is far more interested in our love than in our deeds.

What is done with love and for love's sake, with the firm assurance that it pleases the beloved, is done devotedly. The burden is scarcely felt. When good friends meet each other, heart speaks to heart, and they find joy in each other. So too, whoever is seized by the heartfelt love of Jesus turns to him with joy, and is happy to thank him and praise him.

When one truly venerates the Sacred Heart, it is unthinkable to consider Sunday Mass as a mere "exercise of duty." It is, rather, an immeasurable privilege to be near to the Lord, to be assured of his coming to us in love. It is a supreme joy to join Christ so intimately in the praise of his Father.

Liturgy is marked by this joyous praise of God, but this does not mean that we need no longer pay special attention to our own personal love of Jesus' heart. Liturgy needs the joy that comes from the depths of our hearts, nourished by the heartfelt love of Jesus.

How great must be our joy when we experience, in faith, the ineffable love with which Jesus contacts us— in the Eucharist and in so many other saving signs of redemption. The dynamics of the life of the Church and of our own lives bring us closer to the Lord. This is our abiding and ever-increasing joy.

This eucharistic, thankful, and joyous love of Jesus transforms all our lives into a happy pilgrimage to our eternal home, with the Lord leading us toward a hope-filled homecoming. Friendship with Jesus here on earth is both a "being with" and a "living with" Christ; it establishes a wholesome tension between the now and the not yet. Christ has taken hold of us. He draws us closer to his heart. The initial joy, great as it is, makes us look forward to its fulfillment when heart will repose in heart forever.

## Prayer

*In spite of our sinfulness and weakness, we have enough reasons to be consoled, even to rejoice; for we can still praise you, dearest Lord. It is right that we weep because of our sins, but it is more fitting to rejoice because even our past sins tell us to praise your merciful love with all our hearts because you have forgiven us. Our very pain— that we came so late to love you—is one more sign that you do not take away from us your loving kindness.*

*All of creation and the whole history of salvation tell us of your great love for us. The joyful and serene countenances of people who love you tell us with no need for words. Jesus, thank you for allowing us so often to meet people who, in the midst of most painful suffering, radiate joy and peace—people who so convincingly invite others to praise you. You offer your love as source of joy and peace to all who sincerely seek you. O divine Physician, heal us of all self-induced sadness. May we drink joyfully from your springs of salvation!*

*Lord, let your countenance shine upon us! Send us your light and your truth. Make us wise enough to seek joy at the purest fountain, your heart.*

*We are thirsty for your love, and we come to you. Let us drink as you promised, so that streams of living water will flow from within us. Send us your Holy Spirit and make us joyous messengers of your blissful love!*

# Source *of Our* Love

*When Christ came into the world, he said, "Sacrifices and offerings you have not desired, but a body you have prepared for me; in burnt offerings and sin offerings you have taken no pleasure. Then I said, 'See, God, I have come to do your will, O God'"* (Hebrews 10:5-7a).

At the time when Christ came upon the scene, the great world religions and the mainstreams of philosophy showed great disdain for the human body. Early Christianity had to face this problem. In answer, the biblical texts are strong and clear. Christ's true humanity, including its bodily dimension, belongs to the foundations of our faith. The dignity of the human body appears both in Christ's sacrifice on the cross and in his Resurrection.

Bodily reality has much to do with the worship of God *"in spirit and truth"* (John 4:24). God is spirit, but God's glory shines in visible works, of which the human body is a masterpiece, the embodiment of spirit. In their bodily reality, people are to manifest visibly their being created in the image and likeness of God. In Jesus, the body and its physical heart become absolutely privileged realities in the work of redemption.

On the cross, Jesus reveals himself as embodied freedom in the act of supreme love and trust. He offers his life—"his body" in biblical language—as the greatest gift received from the Father, and as the greatest offering to be brought to the Father for all humankind. In the hour of his death, Jesus' body becomes the real Temple wherein God is adored, and his loving heart is the "Holiest of Holies" in this Temple.

Through his battered body, his heart widely opened for us, Jesus makes visible and tangible his love for us and for his Father. Nailed on the cross, his arms reach out for all. This body, this heart builds bridges between heaven and earth, between person and person.

This crucified body is the acceptable sacrifice, not because of the bitter pains it has to suffer, but because of the love which shines through even in this cruel death. It is "the body given up for us," and Jesus wants every believer, throughout the ages, to remember and to come into contact with this body.

After having served in the work of redemption, Jesus' body is not hidden away. It is raised to glory. It is the perennial gift to the Father, and at the same time a gift to all believers. In his body, Jesus has fullness of life. Giving up his body for us, he receives the greatest glory, which shines in it eternally. So he can say: *"I am the resurrection and the life. Those who believe in me, even though they die, will live"* (John 11:25).

We are "the body of Christ." This paradigm has rich and realistic meaning. We enter into the covenant between Christ and his Church with our full bodily reality: not only with intellect, memory, and will but also with affections, feelings, and emotions. All these dimensions are "embodied."

The body of Christ—having become the real Temple—embraces all of us who are members of the Body of Christ, the Church. In all our dimensions, especially in our bodies, we are consecrated in and through Christ's sacrificial body. *It is by God's will*

*that we have been sanctified through the offering of
the body of Jesus Christ once for all* (Hebrews 10:10).

The human body is not just united with a soul.
People are spirited, being the very expression and evidence of the spiritual dimension. The redeemed are
intact, having gained an integral wholeness. In Jesus,
the integrated wholeness of body, soul, and spirit has
become love incarnate. Christ's body is itself the revelation of God's love.

*Do you not know that you are God's temple and
that God's Spirit dwells in you? If anyone destroys
God's temple, God will destroy that person. For God's
temple is holy, and you are that temple* (1 Corinthians
3:16-17). As Christians, then, we cannot separate our
persons into spheres and parts, bodies and souls. And
when we speak of the love of Jesus, we cannot
abstract it from his bodily heart: The heart is always
the symbol of the center of one's being, and thus of
wholeness and integration. The whole person is to
become embodied love.

## Prayer

*Most loving Savior, from your first to last breath
and heartbeat you considered and honored your
body as a gift of God. All your bodily life, and
especially your sensitive heart, praised your
Father. Your battered body was the most admirable prayer of total abandonment into the hands
of God, a prayer for us.*

*Now we look up to your glorified body, yearning
to find our beatitude in its splendor and to
contemplate it in all eternity. We see your heart as
the fountain of love for heaven and earth. Heaven
has no need for a splendid temple; your body is
the beauty that delights all saints. Your heart is the
Holiest of Holies in this eternal temple.*

*The loving heart of your glorified body draws us to
you. There we have the firmest promise of eternal
life. Help us, by the power of your Spirit, to honor
our own and our neighbors' bodies as temples of
the Holy Spirit, to be invested totally in the service
of adoring and serving love.*

*With great trust we look to your heart and ask you
to enlighten and strengthen us with your grace.
Grant us the wisdom to use all the noble faculties
of our souls and all the energies of our bodies in
your service and for the benefit of the redeemed.*

# Source *of Our* Faith

*Though they knew God, they did not honor him as God or give thanks to him, but they became futile in their thinking, and their senseless minds were darkened. Claiming to be wise, they became fools....And since they did not see fit to acknowledge God, God gave them up to a debased mind and to things that should not be done. They were filled with every kind of wickedness, evil, covetousness, malice. Full of envy, murder, strife, deceit, craftiness, they are gossips, slanderers, God-haters, insolent, haughty, boastful, inventors of evil, rebellious toward parents, foolish, faithless, heartless, ruthless* (Romans 1:21-22, 28-31).

Godlessness spreads in many forms. On the existential level, we become godless when we sever ourselves from the love of God. We radicalize this alienation when we also theoretically deny the God who is Love. A society whose members are heartless and without pity has become godless even before the existence of God is denied.

There are many gods which separate the human person from God: self-glorification which leads to explicit refusal to adore a personal God, arrogance, lust for power, terrorism, senseless arms races, and merciless consumerism that inflicts cruel injustices on the rest of humanity.

Add to this shocking picture the hidden atheism in the hearts and conduct of many people who call themselves Christians, while their thinking and lifestyles are contaminated and largely directed by practical and theoretical atheism.

Only living faith in the God of Love, who has been revealed in Jesus, can destroy these false gods and unmask the various forms of godlessness. Only if our inmost being is filled with the message of love and its transforming grace, and if we turn wholeheartedly to this love which is symbolized in the heart of Jesus, can we guard our hearts and build in the world around us effective dams against this threatening flood of godlessness.

In the present world situation, Christian faith calls more than ever for firm resolution, a radical option for the reign of love. We become credible witnesses insofar as this option takes hold of our whole being, our thoughts, desires, affections, memories, and wills.

Jesus made known to his disciples the tender and strong love for which God sent him into the world. It is also in view of this mission, which he entrusts to us, that he wants to draw us to his heart and fill us with his love, so that we can bring it into the world. Jesus sends us out with and for the same love which he has revealed: *"I made your name known to them, and I will make it known, so that the love with which you have loved me may be in them, and I in them"* (John 17:26).

Only a heart glowing with Christ-like love can effectively repel all forms of hidden and open atheism. Only such a love can unmask all disguises of unbelief, and only the greatest love can find the remedies which humankind needs so desperately in this era of unbelief and godlessness. At this crucial decision-making time in history, all who are captured by the heartfelt love of Christ must join hands and hearts for a common witness to faith bearing fruit in love and justice.

## Prayer

*O heart full of love, O kindly light and fiery flame,
you have come to heal the wounded world, and
for this you set fire to the earth, desiring that it be
kindled. For this confused world, you are also the
sign which forces each of us to make our own
choice. The outcome you desire, and that you
make possible by grace, is the reign of peace and
salvation, a result of faithful love in harmony
with the honor of the heavenly Father.*

*Lord, we want firmly and forever to love you with
all our heart, and we are ashamed that in the past
we have been inconsistent and halfhearted.
Looking at your loving heart, we begin to realize
the magnitude of this injustice to your love and
majesty. If we but love with half a heart, we fail to
fully acknowledge you as our God. This is also a
terrible injustice to humankind, which is so much
in need of credible witnesses.*

*O faithful heart of Jesus, change us, enlighten and
strengthen us in this time of disunity. Help us to
join together in strong faith and faithful love, so
that the world may believe and find the truth of
life. We know that an infinitely merciful God has
infinite love for all creatures. O Lord, free the
godless from their misery and emptiness.*

*Beloved Savior, it is frightening to observe that so
many Christians are apathetic and slothful.
Awaken us all, fill us with new zeal and enthusiasm and show us the most effective ways to
proclaim our faith in you.*

# Source *of Our* Peace

*Let the peace of Christ rule in your hearts, to which indeed you were called in the one body. And be thankful. Let the word of Christ dwell in you richly; teach and admonish one another in all wisdom; and with gratitude in your hearts sing psalms, hymns, and spiritual songs to God* (Colossians 3:15-16).

Configuration of the hearts of believers to the heart of Jesus is made known by the fruits of the Spirit: *The fruit of the Spirit is love, joy, peace, patience, kindness, generosity, faithfulness, gentleness, and self-control* (Galatians 5:22-23). "Love, joy, and peace" form the core, the heart of this rich harvest. All the other distinctive qualities of the redeemed are signs of a peaceful heart and serve as the armor of peacemakers.

The first inalienable condition for our peace mission is to make Christ's peace the arbiter in our hearts. Each of us, according to our charism, capacity, and state in life, is meant to work as peacemaker with all our competence and persistence.

Those who believe in the Beatitudes as saving rules in God's reign are drawn powerfully to the heart of Jesus when they understand his promise: *"Blessed are the peacemakers, for they will be called children of God"* (Matthew 5:9). By being wholly one with Christ, and totally dedicated to his mission as Reconciler, we are sons and daughters along with the only Son of God.

Christ in person is our reconciliation and peace. In him, the saving plan of God, the design for peace, is revealed and fulfilled. But we can call for peace and serve the cause of peace among all people only when our hearts are turned wholly to God.

As a result of this, there develops the eminent art of nonviolent commitment to peace and to peaceful solutions of conflicts. This trust in our inner resources is recommended by Saint Paul: *"I myself feel confident about you, my brothers and sisters, that you yourselves are full of goodness, filled with all knowledge, and able to instruct one another"* (Romans 15:14). But Paul also points to the art of actually mobilizing these resources: *Do not repay anyone evil for evil, but take thought for what is noble in the sight of all. If it is possible, so far as it depends on you, live peaceably with all.... "If your enemies are hungry, feed them; if they are thirsty, give them something to drink; for by doing this you will heap burning coals on their heads." Do not be overcome by evil, but overcome evil with good.* (Romans 12:17-18, 20-21).

The purpose of nonviolent action in the face of conflict is not to destroy our adversary. On the contrary, it is based on the trust that the other person can become a friend, a friend of truth, justice, and peace. Such trust is authentic and efficacious if it is grounded in God.

## Prayer

*We praise you, Lord of heaven and earth, for having sent us your beloved Son, Jesus Christ, to be our reconciliation and our peace. We cherish your thoughts of peace, which you have revealed in Jesus.*

*We firmly believe that you intend to give us the fullness of your peace, since you have sent the One who is our Peace. We thank you for the wisdom of peace in our hearts and for our vocation to be peacemakers, thus proving that we truly are your children. We thank you also for having given us men and women who radiate peace and are wholly dedicated to the cause of peace and reconciliation.*

*Merciful God, in Jesus' name we implore you to forgive us our many sins against peace and our negligence in fostering it. Grant us, as a sign of your forgiveness, a burning zeal and constant faithfulness in promoting the cause of peace in our hearts, in our families and communities, in our Church, and in the entire world. Let there be peace among the nations, in justice and mutual respect.*

*O heart of our Redeemer, fountain of salvation and love, you have consecrated yourself totally to peace, to the glory of your Father and for our salvation. Together with you, we want to consecrate ourselves anew to the cause of peace. When you consecrated yourself before your death, you took us, your disciples, into that all-embracing consecration. Lord, accept our renewed consecration. Grant us your Spirit, so that we may be consecrated in truth. May all our life bear fruit in love, joy, and peace.*

*Amen*